Simone F. de Melo
Glória Maria L. de S. Melo

Childhood and its multiple languages:

Simone F. de Melo
Glória Maria L. de S. Melo

Childhood and its multiple languages:

Teachers' conceptions of the first stage of Basic Education

ScienciaScripts

This book is a translation from the original published under ISBN 978-620-2-04939-9.

Publisher:
Sciencia Scripts
is a trademark of
Dodo Books Indian Ocean Ltd. and OmniScriptum S.R.L publishing group

120 High Road, East Finchley, London, N2 9ED, United Kingdom
Str. Armeneasca 28/1, office 1, Chisinau MD-2012, Republic of Moldova, Europe
Printed at: see last page
ISBN: 978-620-7-24368-6

SUMMARY

To the teachers who work in Early Childhood Education, especially those who give children the opportunity to express their multiple languages.

"If I were to teach a child the beauty of music, I wouldn't start with scores, notes and staves. We'd listen to the best melodies together and I'd tell them about the instruments that make music.

Then, enchanted by the beauty of music, she herself would ask me to teach her the mystery of those black dots written on five lines. Because the black dots and the five lines are just tools for the production of musical beauty. The experience of beauty has to come first. "

Rubem Alves.

SUMMARY

The main objective of this work was to analyze the conceptions of language presented by teachers who work in public institutions of Early Childhood Education - the first stage of Basic Education. In addition to these conceptions, we analyzed the discourse of these teachers in relation to their pedagogical practices regarding the exploration and use of languages by children. For these analyses, we relied on theoretical perspectives recognized as interactionist, which consider language to be a social, historical and cultural product. These include the studies carried out by Vygotsky (1987) and Tomasello (2003). We start from the understanding that language is not just restricted to the child's use of speech, but to all forms of communication and expression that carry meanings, or are made up of signs, such as the language of the body, images, among others (FRANÇOIS, 2006). In this sense, in interactive contexts, in school environments, from Early Childhood Education onwards, a gesture, a drawing, a cry or a look can be considered language. Teachers and their pedagogical practices can be considered important in exploring these forms of communication, which are often observed in contexts of joint attention (MELO, 2015). This is a research project developed through the Scientific Initiation Program (PIBIC), characterized as quantitative and qualitative in nature, whose field of investigation was two public Early Childhood Education institutions, located in the municipalities of Alagoa Nova and Campina Grande, both in the state of Paraiba - Brazil. The subjects involved were teachers who work with children aged 0 to 3 in these institutions. Questionnaires with open-ended questions were used to collect the data. To analyze and discuss the data collected, we used Bardin's (1979) method of content analysis. The data shows, among other things, that the concept of language presented by the teachers is related to the pedagogical practices they develop with regard to the child's use of different languages. The study sought to contribute to the debate about the conceptions and uses of languages by teachers in their teaching process, specifically those involved in Early Childhood Education, in order to rethink curricular and pedagogical practices that aim to ensure the child's right to explore and express different languages.

Keywords: Languages; Teaching Concepts and Practices; Early Childhood Education.

1 INTRODUCTION

Childhood offers the chance to play, study, make discoveries, learn, imagine, play, dance and sing without the fear of making mistakes. However, this view of childhood does not accompany the history of humanity. Studies by Ariès (2011) on the construction of the feeling of childhood, and by Sarmento (2007), who analyzes the process of (in)visibility suffered by children over the years, can be considered references when we propose to discuss childhood in centuries that preceded us, with a view to better understanding this stage of life today, especially when we identify it through its own diverse languages in its development process.

The acquisition and development of language is part of the child's development. In this way, we have tried to briefly discuss the acquisition and development of language through the ideas of Vygotsky (1987) and Tomasello (2003), as both consider language to be a social, historical and cultural product. These ideas contribute to an understanding of the multiple languages that children use in their interactions.

Initially, we need to clarify that we support the idea that language is not restricted to the child's use of speech, but to all forms of communication and expression that carry meaning or are made up of signs, such as the language of the body, images, among others (FRANÇOIS, 2006). In interactive contexts, in school environments, from Early Childhood Education onwards, a gesture, a drawing, a cry or a look can be considered language. Teachers and their pedagogical practices can be considered important in exploring these forms of communication, which are notoriously observed in contexts of joint attention (MELO, 2015). Thus, we consider the following to be part of multiple languages: movement, music, dance, drawing, playing, among others, because any means by which children can express themselves, and which carries meaning, can be considered a language.

The main objective of this work was to analyze the conceptions of language presented by teachers who work in Early Childhood Education - the first stage of Basic Education. We sought to analyze the discourse of these teachers in relation to their pedagogical practices regarding the exploration and use of languages by children. It is important to note that all the teachers who took part in our research work with children aged 0 to 3.

This was a qualitative research project developed through the Scientific Initiation Program - PIBIC. The field of investigation was some public institutions of Early Childhood Education, located in the municipalities of Alagoa Nova and Campina Grande, both in the state of Paraíba - Brazil. A questionnaire with six open questions was used as a data collection tool. Bardin's (1979) content analysis was used to discuss the data collected. The data revealed shows, among other things, that the conceptions of language put forward by primary school teachers are related to the teaching practices they develop.

Finally, we would like to point out that our work, organized into chapters, includes a literature review, in which we consider childhood from a historical and social perspective; and language, based on studies by Vygotsky and Tomasello. In this same review, we discussed some of the languages (body movements, music, dance, playing, drawing) used by children and explored in school practices. In the remaining chapters, we deal with the methodological aspects of our research, as well as presenting and discussing the results of this investigation.

2. LITERATURE REVIEW

2.1 Childhood: some historical and social considerations

The discussion of the history of childhood is recent, since historical references to childhood were made very late, which is one of the reasons why Philippe Ariès stated that "[...] there was no 'feeling of childhood' until the dawn of modernity. [...]" (SARMENTO, 2007, p.26). We should point out that the research carried out by Ariès was based on works of art that sought to represent the reality of a given era.

Philippe Ariès[1] (2011) has tried, through his research, to show us the prominence of the feeling of childhood over the centuries. The author begins his account from the 12th century, when medieval art "[...] was unaware of childhood or did not try to represent it. [...]" (ARIÈS, 2011, p. 17). He assumes that there was probably no place for childhood at the time. Representations of children in paintings were based on the difference in size, i.e. children's features were the same as those of an adult, with the only difference being their size. Only in the following century were some images of children similar to those of modern sentiment noticed. The first type of representation of children resembling modern sentiment was through the painting of an angel with the appearance of a very young boy. The second would be a model of the Child Jesus or Our Lady as a girl, trying to give more realistic features and representations to the feeling of a child. The third type occurred in the Gothic phase, the representation of the nude child, who began to be portrayed on a large scale.

The author points out that even in the 15th and 16th centuries there were no representations of children alone, but it was possible to observe that they became more frequent in anecdotal paintings. As there was no exclusive depiction of childhood, this led to two ideas: the first, that children were mixed in with adults in everyday life; and the second, that painters liked to paint children for their grace or picturesqueness, "[...]. Of these two ideas, one seems archaic to us: today, as at the end of the 19th century, we have a tendency to separate the world of children from the world of adults. The other idea, on the other hand, heralds the modern sense of childhood. " (ARIÈS, 2011, p.21)

Ariès (2011) states that two new types of representation of childhood emerged in the 15th century: the portrait and the *putto*. He shows us that children only appeared in funerary effigies in the 16th century, not in their own tombs or those of their parents, but in those of their teachers. In the same century, the appearance of the portrait of dead children marked an important moment in the history of the feeling of childhood. According to Ariès (2011, p.23), this portrait "[...] was initially a

---

1 We would like to clarify that the author himself has self-corrected in the preface to his work (second edition), where he apologizes for using the term "discovery" of childhood.

funerary effigy. [The first representations contained both dead and living children in the images of their parents' tombs, and what distinguished them was that the dead children were smaller and carried a cross or skull in their hands. And at the end of this century, it was possible to find records that point to tombs with effigies of isolated children.

Throughout his work, Ariès (2011) explains the contributions of each century to the discovery of childhood, which is now recognized and characterized by the multiple languages that identify it. The author shows that the 17th century was one of the centuries that made the greatest contribution to the evolution of early childhood themes. In that same century, portraits of children alone became common, and from that century onwards, family portraits began to be organized around the child. Also in the 17th century, the genre scene gave the child a privileged place with countless scenes of childhood of a conventional nature. And in the middle of the same century, nudity became something of a strict convention in portraits of children. Finally, Ariès' studies allow us to recognize that the 17th century contributed greatly to the constitution of the concept and feeling of childhood and children.

Ariès' contributions to the history of childhood were of great value in helping us to realize how little this part of life was perceived for many years. However, his studies, as mentioned above, focused on autobiographical references and scattered records that show the presence of children in the past, thus suffering strong criticism, as stated by Sarmento (2007, p.27):

[...] it is often criticized that Ariès theorized about the entire social category of childhood, having used documentary records from the clergy and the nobility, and consequently there was a lack of references to the children of the lower classes [...].

What is being criticized is the fact that Ariès based his entire study on just one class. At no point are we belittling the studies and research carried out by the author. We believe that his studies were a door that opened for new discoveries about childhood to be made, and that there have been more studies and research into the history, sociology and languages of childhood. We understand that the emergence of the emphasis on childhood contributed, among other things, to our being able to perceive children in their different possibilities of communication, through different languages.

Another author who tries to work with the "discoveries" and "concealment" of childhood is Manuel Jacinto Sarmento, *already* mentioned in our work. The author works with the idea of the concealment, revelation and hiding of childhood, depending on the historical context in which the child is involved. He shows us different processes of concealment which he calls (in)visibility, starting with the historical (in)visibility suffered by the child, then civil (in)visibility and finally

7

scientific (in)visibility. We will focus on historical (in)visibility[2].

According to Sarmento (2007), childhood has been subjected to a process of concealment that stems from historically constructed conceptions of children and the ways in which they have been inscribed in social images that "[...] both shed light on their products (the set of structured systems of beliefs, theories and ideas in different historical periods) and conceal the reality of children's social and cultural worlds, in the complexity of their social existence..." (SARMENTO, 2007, p. 26). In this way, childhood goes through several phases of concealment and illumination, in other words, the more we think we know about childhood, the more we realize the lack of knowledge about it.

Sarmento (2007) gives us a historical overview of how this (in)visibility occurred during the industrial revolution, when many children worked in industries as cheap labor, but the *crash of* the New York stock exchange in 1929 led to children experiencing another phase of symbolic exclusion from childhood, that of the economy, where "[...] children were considered to be beings removed from production and consumption, and childhood was invested with the nature of the *non-working age.*" (SARMENTO, 2007, p. 34 - emphasis added).

Sarmento (2007) shows us that in the second modernity, with the active development of a cultural industry aimed at children and the constant emphasis of the media in our children's daily lives, they end up living "[...]definitively a process of early and irreversible adultization, and consequently inhabit the age of *non-childhood*. [...]" (idem). Neil Postman's (1983) conception of childhood exposes the idea of the "death of childhood", which hides the idea of the child's active nature and conceals the fact that children live in the peculiarity of their generation. Sarmento (2007) states that it is "[...] incorrect *(sic) to* speak of the death of childhood, even though contemporary childhood does indeed suffer from powerful constraints and is especially vulnerable to the colonization of its lifeworlds by adults. [...]" (p.35).

The studies carried out by Ariès, Sarmento and other researchers who discuss childhood show us that there is not just one childhood, but several, demythologizing the concept of childhood and showing us childhoods. Since the concept of childhood is given with reference to the society in which the child is living, according to Kuhlmann and Fernandes (2004, p.15), "the history of childhood would then be the history of the relationship of society, culture and adults with this age group, and the history of children among themselves and with adults, with culture and with society". It is worth pointing out that the idea of the child, along with the concept of childhood that

---

2 We chose to discuss historical (in)visibility because we are discussing the history of childhood, and because we are trying, albeit briefly, to make a connection between the ideas of Aries (2011) and Sarmento (2007) from this historical perspective.

we have today, was one of the representations created and rooted in the capitalist system, i.e. "[...] the notion of childhood emerged with capitalist, urban-industrial society, as the insertion and social role of the child in their community changed" (BRASIL, 2006, p.14).

But what differentiates childhood from other stages of life? What makes it such an important and unique phase? Sarmento (2007, p.35) helps us answer this question by stating that:

[...] childhood owes its difference not to the absence of characteristics (presumably) proper to the adult human being, but to the presence of other distinctive characteristics which allow that, beyond all the distinctions made by belonging to different social classes, to the male or female gender, to whatever geographical space they live in, their culture of origin and ethnicity, all children in the world have something in common.

Therefore, this stage of life goes beyond any stereotypes given, it is not limited to the age of non-speech. Every child demonstrates some kind of language, be it gestural, bodily, verbal, dramatic, theatrical, musical, pictographic, among others, simply because they are able to express feelings, emotions; to understand, to mean, to communicate. This is not the non-work phase either. Children have their work to do, be it with their studies, the small domestic activities that their mother assigns them, or even with their games. So childhood is:

[...] simultaneously, a social category, of the generational type, and a social group of active subjects, who interpret and act in the world. In this action, they structure and establish cultural patterns. Children's cultures are, in fact, the most important aspect in differentiating childhood (SARMENTO, 2007, p.36).

What we tried to discuss, in broad strokes, was the historical trajectories of the constitution of the concept of childhood and the perception of the child, so that we can better understand the child today as a social subject, with languages, distinct from the adult, who produces cultures. Discussing languages that are used by children in situations of social interaction, such as those that take place in school environments, requires us to situate ourselves in these paths, understanding our past, so that we can look to the future and start doing things differently.

It is in childhood that children learn to walk, to define their tastes, to show their dissatisfaction, and to understand ways of communicating. It is during this phase that children identify their affections, their family, and create bonds. This is the stage when communication is established, whether through crying, gestures, babbling, gestures or speech itself. And all this learning and forms of communication and expression can be called languages.

2.2 Language from the perspective of Vygotsky and Tomasello

Tomasello (2003, p.4) states that this is due to a biological mechanism that causes changes in behavior and cognition and this mechanism is "[...] social or cultural transmission, which works on

9

time scales of much faster magnitudes than those of organic evolution. [...]". This social or cultural transmission allows each being to appropriate existing knowledge and skills. The author points out that this cultural transmission includes things such as a baby bird imitating the typical song of its species and makes our children acquire "[...] the linguistic conventions of the other members of their social group. [...]" (TOMASELLO, 2003, p.5), in other words, cultural transmission enables us to learn the language used by the social group in which we live.

Based on this assumption, we can see that Tomasello understands that language, and its acquisition, develops through a social process. Along the same lines, i.e. corroborating the social and cultural nature of language, studies by Vygotsky (1987), Wallon (1995) and Bakhtin (1988) stand out. The latter emphasizes the ideological nature of language. All these authors find support in one of the theoretical currents that discuss language, the so-called interactionist current.

We want to emphasize that we consider language not only as a phonic aspect, but something that goes beyond speech, "equivalent to everything that can have a sign and meaning, such as the language of the body or the language of images [...]" (FRANÇOIS, 2006, p.185, *apud,* MELO, 2015 p.20). So a gesture, a drawing, a cry or a look can all be considered languages.

In order to understand Vygotsky's point of view on language, we need to understand the context in which this concept was formed. Vygotsky (1987, p.21) criticizes the main currents and trends in contemporary psychology, claiming that they do not consider the development of the relationship between thought and speech.

A glance at the results of previous research into thought and language will show that all the existing theories, from antiquity to the present day, cover the whole range from the identification and fusion of thought and speech at one end, to an almost metaphysical separation and segregation of the two at the other. [...]

In addition to associationist psychology, he also criticized Gestalt and behaviorist psychology, claiming that when they studied thought and language, they made no reference to the historical process of their development. In this way, Vygotsky's aim, according to Jobin and Souza (1994), was to unite the two halves of psychology in order to,

[...] to create a new system that would synthesize these conflicting ways of studying man, because, for Vygotsky, none of the existing psychological currents provided the firm foundations needed to establish a unified theory of higher psychological processes. [...] (JOBIN E SOUZA, 1994, p.124).

Thus, Vygotsky (1987) ended up founding a psychology called **cultural-historical psychology**, based on historical and dialectical materialism. The method of dialectical historical materialism understands that the object of study must be understood by following the process of movement and change that it has undergone. For this author, "[...] every phenomenon has its history and this history is characterized by qualitative and quantitative changes" (VYGOTSKY, 1984, *apud*, JOBIN E SOUZA, 1994, p.124). Vygotsky emphasized the unique qualities existing in the human species, as well as the transformations and cultural and historical contexts constructed by humanity.

Vygotsky (1987) reformulated Engels' conception of human work and the use of instruments, and "[...] extended this concept of mediation in human-environment interaction through the use of instruments to the use of signs. [...]" (JOBIN E SOUZA, 1994, p.125). In Vygotsky's understanding, signs and instruments are created by society throughout history and change according to its social and cultural reality.

In this way, the phenomenon of language is seen by this author as part of the signs created by society throughout history and within a cultural and social context, which brings about change in the cultural development of society and ends up shaping man himself, who creates it. To reinforce this idea, Lucci (2006, p.5) states that for Vygotsky "the individual is determined in social interactions, that is, it is through the relationship with the other and by itself that the individual is determined; it is in language and by itself that the individual is determined and is determinant of other individuals". Thus, Vygotsky's studies show us that the human being develops in a

A long process marked by qualitative leaps that occur in three stages: from phylogenesis (origin of the species) to sociogenesis (origin of society); from sociogenesis to ontogenesis (origin of man) and from ontogenesis to microgenesis (origin of the single individual) (LUCCI, 2006, p.5).

The socio-historical theory, a current that presents Vygotsky's ideas, emphasizes that human development originates from two distinct lines: "an elementary process, biologically based, and a higher process of sociocultural origin" (LUCCI, 2006, p.7). Thus, this theory "starts from the conception that all organisms are active and establishes a continuous interaction between social conditions, which are mutable, and the biological basis of human behavior".

According to Melo (2015, p.25) Vygotsky "[...] constructed a theory that could explain the origin and evolution of human consciousness, that is, the evolution of man's higher psychological structures in his development process". This construction took place through a critical analysis of the theoretical perspectives present at the time. In Vygotsky's conception, it is through language, in interactional contexts, that the development of higher psychological structures occurs. Thus, development is associated with the child's ability to acquire language, throughout their insertion in contexts of social interaction, between children and adults or between children themselves, in which they use a given language, or other forms of expression and communication.

The development of higher psychic functions is interconnected with the mediation between man and the environment, whether cultural or social. According to Oliveira (2002, p. 26), Vygotsky's concept of mediation "[...] in general terms is the process of an intermediary element intervening in

11

a relationship; the relationship then ceases to be direct and becomes mediated by this element." Furthermore, Oliveira (2002, p. 33) adds that:

The process of mediation, through instruments and signs, is fundamental to the development of higher psychological functions, distinguishing man from other animals. Mediation is an essential process for making voluntary, intentional psychological activities possible, controlled by the individual himself.

In this way, mediation takes place for the development of higher psychic functions to occur, for example, in a process of social interaction, where languages are used to grasp new content from this environment. This apprehension takes place through a process called *internalization* by Vygotsky, which begins first in the social and then individually, as Jobim and Souza (1994, p. 125;126) state:

The internalization of historically determined and culturally organized content therefore takes place mainly through language, thus making it possible for people's social nature to also become their psychological nature [...] In the child's cultural development, every function appears twice: first at the social level and later at the individual level. This process of internalization, that is, the transformation of an interpersonal process into an intrapersonal process, involves the use of signs and involves a complex evolution in which a series of qualitative transformations occur in the child's consciousness.

Discussing the Vygotsky perspective on language, Melo (2015, p. 24) points out that the social contexts in which children use language drive not only communication, but also the internalization of this content, which occurs through the use of signs. It is in this process of internalization that a transformation can take place in the child's consciousness, which starts from a thought constructed in a group (social), to later become a thought of a psychological nature (individual). Thus, for Melo (2015, p. 24), "[...] language, in this process, is acquired in the context of social interactions in the use of words, and then constructed in the context of individual cognitive processes. [...]".

Vygotsky analyzes the relationship between thought and language, which he calls "unit analysis" (VYGOTSKY, 2005, p. 5, *apud,* MELO, 2015, p.25). He sought to analyze this relationship as a whole, that is, without distinguishing the sound from the meaning of words, thus considering the whole of verbal thought and the meanings of words. Thus, "[...] it is in the meaning of words that thought and speech unite in verbal thought. It is in meaning, Vygotsky emphasizes, that answers can be found to the relationship between thought and speech. [...] (MELO, 2015, p.25). This relationship between thought and speech takes place within a dynamic process.

In his studies investigating the relationship between thought and speech in the early stages, Vygotsky (1987) states that there is no interdependence between the genetic roots of thought and speech. With this, he shows that the relationship between thought and speech is not a precondition for the development of human consciousness, but a product of it. Thus, for Vygotsky, the relationship between thought and speech is "[...] a process with distinct genetic roots, but which, throughout the evolution of both, establish a continuous and systematic interdependence between them that changes and develops. [...]" (JOBIM E SOUZA, 1994, p. 127).

For Vygotsky, thought and speech are not linked by a primary link. Thought initially evolves without language. In this sense, again using Jobim and Souza's (1994, p. 128) interpretation of Vygotsky's thinking, "[...] the child's first babbles are a form of communication without thought [...]". Thus, in Vygotsky's understanding, there is a pre-integral thought, since the child tries to attract the adult's attention through various sounds, and communicates its sensations through pleasure and displeasure, and it is up to the mother, or another adult with an affective bond with the child, to decode these sensations.

According to Jobim and Souza (1994, p. 128), Vygotsky's (1987) studies show that the junction of pre-linguistic thought and pre-intellectual language occurs around the age of two:

[...] the crucial moment occurs around the age of six, when the curves of pre-linguistic thought and pre-intellectual language meet and come together, initiating a new type of organization of thought and language. At this point, thought becomes verbal and speech rational. [...]

For Vygotsky (1987), the study of the transition from thought to speech can be done by analyzing the ontogenetic development of language. But for this to happen, it is necessary to understand the two levels of verbal language: the internal aspect of verbal language (semantic and meaningful) and the external aspect (sound). Although the semantic and phonetic aspects form a single unit, each has its own laws of movement. Through this study, Vygotsky (1987) concludes that thought and speech do not come from a single model; on the contrary, each has more differences than similarities, but this is what guarantees the dialectical unity between thought and speech.

Vygotsky (1987) tried to understand the psychological nature of inner speech, admitting Piaget's pioneering work on this topic, but claiming that he failed to grasp the most important characteristic of egocentric speech. For this author, the speech of children between the ages of two and seven has two functions which they cannot dissociate: the internal function (coordinating and directing thought) and the external function (communicating the results to other people). For Vygotsky (1987), "egocentric speech arises when the child transfers social and cooperative forms of behavior to the sphere of inner and personal psychic functions" (JOBIM E SOUZA, 1994, p.132). Egocentric speech plays a fundamental role in the child's development, and is a period of transition from interpsychic to intrapsychic functions. For him, it is a phase that precedes the child's inner speech.

Tomasello (2003) shares the same ideas as Vygotsky (1987). Tomasello (2003) states that language acquisition occurs at the junction of the biological and the sociocultural, defending in his studies that the process of language acquisition and development is found in the "theory of language acquisition based on use" or in "cognitive-functional linguistics" (TOMASELLO, 2003). According

13

to Allan and Souza (2009, p.161), the central hypothesis of this theory is that the acquisition of language is a process of development.

[...] and the development of human linguistic competences are socio-biological processes involving human socio-cognitive skills of understanding and sharing intentionality and participation in historically established socio-communicative activities with linguistically and symbolically competent human individuals.

In this way, it is possible to establish a relationship with the ideas of Vygotsky (1987) and Tomasello (2003), since both consider that the process of language acquisition and development is based on biological and sociocultural principles, so that man learns and develops language within a sociocultural environment which has a history that is inherited by him and which, at the same time, changes over time, and there is always an intentionality. Thus, theories of language acquisition based on use propose that "[...] human cognition is the co-evolutionary product of specific biological adaptations to primate cognition and collaborative activities related to cultural cognition. [...]" (ALLAN and SOUZA, 2009, p.162).

One of the important concepts for understanding the process of language acquisition and development in Tomasello is that of *intentionality* and *causality*. Tomasello (2003, p.25) defends the idea that non-human primates do not understand the intentionality of specific co-beings and the causality of inanimate objects and events, stating that "[...] non-human primates are intentional and causal beings, only they do not understand the world in intentional and causal terms". For the author, it is the understanding of intentionality and causality that differentiates us from non-human primates.

[...] the uniquely human ability to understand external events in relation to intentional/causal mediating forces first emerged in human evolution to enable individuals to predict and explain the behavior of co-specifics and was later transposed to deal with the behavior of inert objects. (TOMASELLO, 2003, p.33)

According to Àllan and Souza (2009, p.163), in a study of Tomasello's ideas and conceptions, there is another factor which would be the "uniquely human motivation to share intentionality with other human individuals". So it would be the motivation to show what one has discovered or learned to someone else that makes us beings with shared intentionality. For Tomasello (2003), the advantages of having causal intentional thinking are twofold. The first is that this type of thinking enables us to solve problems in creative, flexible and persistent ways, thus, "[...] the causal and intentional understanding of humans therefore has immediate consequences for effective action, in that it opens up the possibility of finding new ways of manipulating or suppressing mediating forces" (TOMASELLO, 2003, p. 34). The second would be the fact that intentional/causal understanding enables a transformative function in the social learning process.

[...]. In other words, understanding other people's behavior as intentional and/or mental makes certain very

14

powerful forms of cultural learning and sociogenesis directly possible, and these forms of social learning are directly responsible for the special forms of cultural inheritance characteristic of human beings. [...] (TOMASELLO, 2003, p. 34).

Another concept used by Tomasello (2003) to understand the process of language acquisition and development is that of cumulative cultural evolution, which the author also calls the ratchet effect. This cumulative cultural evolution would be the modifications made by different individuals over time to one (or several) objects or even to the language itself, making it more complex and comprehensive with adaptive aspects and functions. In another paper developed with collaborators, Tomasello et al. state that this evolution occurs basically through learning by imitation. Their argument is that,

[...] cumulative cultural evolution depends on two processes - innovation and imitation (probably supplemented by instruction) - which have to occur in a dialectical process over time so that one step in the process leads to the next. (TOMASELLO, 2003, p.53).

For Tomasello (2003), the fact that we human beings are able to accumulate and modify our cultural traditions over time, and that these traditions have their own "histories" and that we know them, distinguishes them from the cultural traditions presented by chimpanzees. The author states that this process of accumulating modifications and having a history in the cultural learning system becomes particularly powerful because it is based on uniquely human cognitive adaptations to understand others as intentional agents equal to oneself, which create forms of social learning that act like a ratchet, and which preserve newly created strategies in the social group until a new innovation can replace them.

To end these comparisons that many researchers try to make about the process of culture accumulation between human beings and chimpanzees, Tomasello (2003, p.55) points out that the difference would be that "[...] human beings usually have the socio-cognitive and cultural learning capacities to create, as a species, unique cognitive products based on cumulative cultural evolution".

Tomasello (2003) presents two basic forms of sociogenesis that can be found in human societies, which enable the creation of something new through the social interaction of two or more individuals in cooperative interaction. The first would be precisely the ratchet effect described above; the second would be the collaboration of two or more individuals to solve a problem. Tomasello (2003) also shows us where we can find examples of cumulative cultural evolution, citing the sociogenesis of language and mathematics.

In the sociogenesis of language, Tomasello (2003) argues that the sharing of linguistic symbols between individuals who use a particular language to communicate enables a symbolic socialization of their experiences and leads to a better way of using these symbols, thus enabling a historical and

15

dynamic evolution of the language used in human communication.

[...] All the symbols and constructions of a given language were not invented all at once, and once invented they generally do not remain identical for long. On the contrary, linguistic symbols evolve, change and accumulate modifications over historical time as people use them among themselves [...] (TOMASELLO, 2003, p.58).

With this in mind, Melo (2015, p.41) says that it is possible to affirm that, from birth onwards, when children begin their process of interaction with the socio-cultural environment, whether through their parents or caregivers, they share in the historical and cultural modifications of language, as well as acting as the subject of this process, contributing to its evolution. Therefore,

[...] it is only when the child begins to perceive himself and the other as an intentional agent, according to Tomasello (2003), that one can observe this action that characterizes changes in linguistic structures, moving from simpler forms to complex forms, which enable users of a given language, according to their cultures, to share symbols and communicate. For this scholar, it is the cultural differences between peoples that characterize the particularities of languages (MELO, 2015, p.41-42).

Thus, we can understand that language, for Tomasello, is a universal cognitive process, being a result of biological inheritances, which are elaborated and modified according to their practices of use and sociocultural developments, thus being based on "[...] universally human ways of experiencing the world (...) and on some processes of cultural creation and sociogenesis" (TOMASELLO, 2003 p. 61).

Following this principle, we can find conditions for the acquisition of language by the child, taking into account that from birth, in its ontogenetic process, "[...] it begins the development of its intellectual abilities in the interaction with the environment, with the other and, therefore, with the socio-cultural and historical resources available [...]" (MELO, 2015, p.42). And it is precisely in these contexts, according to Tomasello, that we can find the cognitive abilities for language, which are universally available.

The place where intellectual needs meet directly with cultural resources is undoubtedly human ontogenesis. Indeed, sociogenesis and cultural history can be understood as a series of ontogeneses in which mature and immature members of a culture learn to act efficiently [...]. The most basic cognitive skills necessary for language acquisition [...] are universally available to human beings (TOMASELLO, 2003 p.65).

We know that Tomasello considers both the historical process in the realization of language and the interaction with the environment (individual and cultural lines) for the child's development. Basically, these two lines meet in two processes: imitation and creation.

To the extent that children appropriate the cultural conventions they have learned through imitation or some other form of cultural learning, they make a creative leap that goes beyond them and deduce, on their own, some categorical or analogical relationship (TOMASELLO, 2003, p.72).

In this understanding, we can understand that cultural inheritance or cultural learning, according to Tomasello (2003, p.71) "focuses on intentional phenomena in which an organism adopts the behavior or perspective of another in relation to a third entity". In this way, according to Melo (2015, p.43) we should understand how important cultural conventions are, "[...] or the cultural activities socially shared between children [...] and more experienced adults [...]", because as this process matures, the child not only appropriates the culture already produced, but can creatively rework it and establish new relationships and draw up their own deductions.

It is worth noting that despite considering both processes (biological and cultural), Tomasello (2003, p.70-71) makes a distinction between the lines of biological inheritance and cultural inheritance. According to the author, this distinction occurs as follows,

The *individual line of* cognitive development concerns those things that the organism knows and learns on its own without direct influence from other people or their artifacts, while the *cultural line of* cognitive development concerns those things that the organism knows and learns through acts in which it tries to see the world through the perspective of other people (emphasis added).

Although the individual line, presented in Tomasello's distinction, appears to be a development that occurs autonomously, it doesn't seem clear that it develops without the influence of the cultural line, since the child learns a language according to the culture in force in the place where they were born. Thus, for Melo (2015, p.42), language acquisition,

From this perspective, perhaps it represents more than the interaction of these lines: perhaps a complementarity between the human cognitive capacity for apprehension/learning and the child's interactive experience in the socio-cultural world. For, according to Tomasello himself (2003, p. 131), "language is a symbolically incorporated social institution that has historically emerged from pre-existing sociocommunicative activities". From this perspective, the child's use of language seems to be an important impetus and even an important condition for acquiring and mastering language.

One of the key points for understanding human cognition and the ontogenesis presented by Tomasello is the importance of intentionality for human development. However, we have to understand that the understanding of intentional action "[...] although considered a biological adaptation in Tomasello's model, does not emerge immediately or fully developed immediately after the birth of a human baby. [...]" (ALLAN and SOUZA, 2009, p.163). In other words, intentionality is a gradual process which involves the organization of the human baby's sensory-motor actions, identification with its co-specifics, and its actual formation, which should occur around nine months of life.

Àllan and Souza (2009) discuss three levels of understanding intentional action during human

17

ontogenetic development, elaborated by Tomasello et al:

a)   *Understanding animated action.* Around the age of six months, children begin to understand their co-specifiers as being capable of spontaneous action and can follow their direction of action and construct their own experiences in terms of action in familiar contexts. One aspect of the child's behavior during this period is their daily relationship with the physical and social environment;

b)   *Understanding goal-oriented action.* At nine months of age, children begin to show a pattern of social cognition that is different from that of non-human primates. They begin to realize that their co-specifics are capable of performing specific actions and producing specific goals.

c)   *Understanding action planning.* At around fourteen months of age, children understand that their co-specifiers are capable of selecting action plans to produce goals in specific contexts. They are also able to engage in forms of cultural learning, predicting the actions of their co-specifics and learning to do things established in their culture.

Continuing the studies by Tomasello, Àllan and Souza (2009), it is stated that during the first year of children's lives, in addition to developing the skills to understand intentional action and the motivation to share intentionality, they also begin to share certain aspects of their own experience with adults. These forms of interaction between children and adults (shared intentionality) are characterized by three levels: *Dyadic engagement.* Occurring around the age of six months, children begin to share actions and emotional states with their co-species; *Triadic engagement*[3] . At nine months, children share their goals, actions and perceptions with their co-species; *Collaborative engagement.* Between the ages of fourteen months, children share intentional states and perceptions with their co-species, taking joint action to achieve the shared goal. It is through collaborative engagement that children experience unique situations of social interaction, cultural learning, symbolic communication and cognitive representation.

Regarding collaborative engagement, Àllan and Souza (2009, p. 164) state that "[...] children learn to internalize, in the form of dialogical cognitive representations, the perspectives of adults and to use them to mediate their understanding of the world and human culture. [...]".

For a better understanding of the three levels of intentional action and shared intentionality, we have reproduced a table presented by the authors, which was drawn up by Tomasello and colleagues (figure 1). The first table shows the three levels of understanding of intentional action. The second table shows the motivation for sharing intentionality. The third table shows the levels of shared intentionality. And finally, the age group the child is in.

---

3 Melo (2015), in a study of social interactions of joint attention between teachers and children in the process of language acquisition, identified another type of interaction, which he called *quadratic interaction* (emphasis added).

18

The concepts presented in this table are extremely important for understanding joint attention, especially triadic and collaborative engagements. By engaging triadically and collaboratively with adults, children begin to experience scenes of joint attention.

Figure 1 - Schematic of the development of the understanding of intentional action and shared intentionality during the first year of a child's life

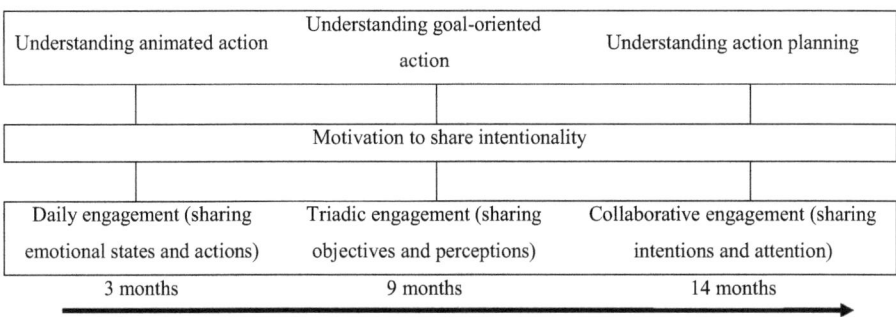

Source: (Tomasello & cols., 2005, *apud*, Àllan and Souza, 2009, p.164)

They were presented because Tomasello (2013) states that joint attention is of fundamental importance for language acquisition. In his studies he defines this

These are "social interactions in which the child and adult jointly pay attention to a third thing, and to each other's attention to the third thing, for a reasonable period of time" (TOMASELLO, 2003, p.135). Thus, they are interactions that involve mutual coordination of both the adult and the child towards a jointly observed element (Idem).

We know that children learn both in situations with an adult, with another child and with themselves, so children are constantly learning and developing. As we have already explained, even before they acquire the ability to communicate verbally, children are able to express themselves/communicate with the members of their culture through actions and gestures, so they end up developing communicative tools. These communicative tools can be called multiple languages that are developed and expressed by the child.

2.3 Multiple languages

We began our discussion by presenting the creation and evolution of the feeling of childhood and the (in)visibility that children suffered (suffer) during certain periods of our history. We then approached some of the theoretical perspectives that discuss language in the light of Tomasello (2003) and Vygotsky (1987). We have done all this because we believe that the multiple languages used by children, and best observed in school teaching practices, are interconnected with their process of language development and acquisition, in other words, the process of learning a language and using speech.

19

Considering that children don't only use oral language to communicate, and that this multiplicity of languages is present in school practices and sometimes constitutes them, we carried out our research with teachers who work with children in Early Childhood Education, more specifically with children aged between 0 and 3, in order to analyze how they consider the various forms of communication and expression they use. It is possible to observe that, from an early age, this communication can be seen through body movements, sounds, music, dance, drawing, etc. Palomo (2001) states that language is a complex system of meaning and communication and can be of two types: **verbal**, whose signs are words, and **non-verbal**, which uses other signs such as images, sounds and gestures. Below we will discuss the multiple languages mentioned by the teachers involved in our research process.

2.3.1 Movement and the child

From before birth, in its mother's womb, the child moves and at birth these movements become constant and throughout its growth will be used to communicate initially with its mother, but as its development progresses new bodily possibilities are appropriated so that an increasingly elaborate interaction occurs with the social world in which it lives.

It is through movement that children "[...] learn about themselves, relate to others and objects, develop their abilities and learn skills. [...]" (GARANHANI, NADOLNY, 2011). In this way, movement is more than just moving the body in space, it's a language that allows children to act on the physical environment, insert themselves into the social environment, express their thoughts and experience relationships with objects and people.

According to Galvao (2008, p. 69) Wallon considers that "[...] in addition to its role in the relationship with the physical world (performing motor skills), movement plays a fundamental role in affectivity and also in cognition [...]".]", in other words, movement is not just about moving the body, it is also a process that uses cognitive and emotional factors to materialize, because when children move, they express feelings, emotions and thoughts, expanding the possibilities of meaningful use of gestures and body postures.

In this way, we see movement as a **language,** because we believe that in an interactive context, movement can be charged with meaning and intention, and thus also considered an important dimension of human development and culture. According to the Referencial Curricular Nacional para a Educaçao Infantil - RCNEI (BRASIL, 1998, vol. 3, p.47),

The ways of walking, running, throwing and jumping are the result of social interactions and human relationships with the environment; they are movements whose meanings have been constructed according to the different needs, interests and human bodily possibilities present in different cultures at different times in history.

20

According to Wallon (1975), before establishing a relationship with the physical environment, movement first acts on the human environment, reaching people through its expressive content. For the author, movement plays a greater role than a mere relationship with the physical world; according to him, it is through movement that children develop cognition and affectivity from birth. The author points out that the primary function of movement is to help children develop their affectivity and that, throughout their development, children begin to relate to the physical world through movement and consequently develop their cognitive dimension.

Wallon (1979) also shows us that in early childhood, the mental act develops into the motor act, in other words, the child thinks when they are doing the action and this means that the movement of the body plays an important role in the early stages of child development. But how does this happen?

For Wallon (1979, p.74) "the organ of movement in all its forms is the striated musculature" and it has two functions: the *kinetic function* and the *tonic function*. The kinetic function is characterized by the stretching and shortening of muscle fibres and makes movement itself possible. The tonic function is characterized by the variation in the level of tension of the muscles in order to maintain body balance and constitutes the attitudes, i.e. the postural reactions. Even in a kinetic activity (the movement itself) the muscles depend on the tonic function and this is necessary to maintain body posture.

[...] The tonic function, which maintains a certain level of tension in the muscle, varies according to the physiological conditions of the subject or the difficulties of the act being performed. It is the tone that keeps the muscles in the shape that gave them the movement, in case the movement is interrupted. It accompanies the movement to support its effort to the extent of the resistance encountered, but it can dissociate itself from it and transform it into a stable attitude, i.e. immobility (WALLON, 1979, p.74-75).

In this way, body balance is regulated by the tonic function, whether in movement or immobility, but its main purpose is the expression of emotions. According to Garanhani (2005, p. 2018), emotions are followed by facial and body mimicry, which are translated into attitudes that have specific meanings according to the culture to which they belong. "Attitudes are therefore related, on the one hand, to the child's accommodation or mobilization in the process of adapting to the environment and, on the other hand, to their emotional life. " However, "this entire functional apparatus is far from being operational from birth. Its components will each appear in their own time, and will then allow the child to modify their relationship with the environment" (WALLON, 1979, p.75).

According to Garanhani (2005), Wallon, when describing the process of child development, points out that the child, at the beginning of his development, establishes relationships of communication

21

with the environment, through the selection of body movements that guarantee his closeness to others and the satisfaction of his needs. In other words, movements initially represent/transmit feelings of well-being or discomfort.

As development progresses, the child's relationship with the environment facilitates the discrimination of ways of communicating, with walking and speech triggering a qualitative leap in early childhood development, enabling greater autonomy and independence in the investigation of space and the objects found in it (GARANHANI, 2005, p.2018).

In this way, movement is one of the first languages used by children to communicate with the social world, which throughout their mental/corporal development new languages are incorporated that generate autonomy and independence for the child, but movement is not forgotten, it develops according to the child's development.

2.3.2 The language of music

Throughout our work we have shown that children use different languages to communicate, get to know each other and appropriate the cultures already present in their social environment. And that this is a long process that begins with contact with the mother, for example, through crying to express what they are feeling, and extends and evolves throughout life in communicative situations present in interpersonal relationships.

Afonso (2011) takes us back in time to the care that was given to newborn children for a long time. They were protected from contact with people and the world, because it was believed that children needed to be protected from noise, colors, light, sound and people themselves, as these interactions could damage their health and their physical and mental well-being.

The author also shows us why these customs have been put aside, one of the reasons being that with the "[...] advancement of research in different fields of knowledge, the appreciation of the child's interaction with the various artistic languages from an early age began. [...] (AFONSO, 2011, p.109) and the defense of some scholars in the idea that the child, even before birth, should be stimulated through music, conversations and other languages, because this contact with these languages would provide the baby, still in the womb, with proximity to art "[...] sensitizing him to the important interactions for his development".

In addition to the facts presented by the actor, we also believe that the growing value placed on public policies for Early Childhood Education has contributed to our children having contact with artistic and bodily languages at an increasingly early age. The result of one of these policies is the RCNEI (BRASIL, 1998). The RCNEI suggests that, in the context of the experience of knowing the world, the axes of work oriented towards the construction of different languages by children and the

22

relationships they establish with the objects of knowledge: movement, music, visual arts, oral and written language, nature, society and mathematics.

With this in mind, we can say that music and dance are languages presented to and learned by children, languages that manifest themselves in different ways and that are interconnected with the culture of the society in which the child is inserted.

According to the Referencial Curricular para a Educação Infantil (BRASIL, 1998, p.45),

Music is the language that translates into sound forms capable of expressing and communicating sensations, feelings and thoughts, through the organization and expressive relationship between sound and silence. Music is present in all cultures, in the most diverse situations: festivals and celebrations, religious rituals, civil and political demonstrations, etc.

So we can see that music is a global, cultural phenomenon that has many faces and is often capable of breaking down barriers that man himself builds. Music makes us get to know new cultures and customs, it can calm us down, relax us and entertain us. In this way, music can only add to the life and learning process of the child and enhance the work of the teacher.

Music needs to be used in early childhood education for a number of reasons. One of these reasons is the fact that many children already have contact with music before they are born. After birth, this contact can occur in family environments, in the church the family attends and throughout their development, in the games they play. According to Souza and Joly (2010, p. 98) "[...] when children play or interact with the sound universe, they end up discovering, even if in a simple way, different ways of making music". Thus, we can say that making music arises according to the play and even according to the situation experienced by the child.

Through play, children relate to the world they discover every day and this is how they make music: by playing. Always receptive and curious, they search for sound materials, invent melodies and listen with pleasure to the music of different peoples and places. (JOLLY, 2003, p. 116)

As we've already mentioned, music is closely linked to culture, and even before a child is born they already have contact with part of this culture. Through this small contact, throughout their development, children begin to broaden their sound senses and get to know part of this culture better, which is linked to their social environment, beginning to identify and develop a connection with the music around them. This is why it takes on different meanings in each culture, because, according to Penna (2008), music is,

[...] a cultural language, we consider familiar that type of music that is part of our experience; precisely because being part of our experience allows us to become familiar with its principles of sound organization, which makes music meaningful to us. (p. 21).

23

And so we become accustomed to and identify with the patterns of sound organization present in our culture, which allows us to establish links with the people, customs and traditions of the place where we live. In this respect, the author states that:

[...] the understanding of music, or even sensitivity to it, is based on a culturally shared pattern for the organization of sounds in an artistic language, a pattern which, socially constructed, is socially apprehended - through experience, daily contact, familiarization - although it can also be learned at school. (PENNA, 2008, p. 29).

With this, we can affirm that working with music can happen in the school environment, as we have already reported. In the RCNEI, specifically volume three, there is a section dedicated to this content. In this document, we can see that musical experience can provide children with the integration of experiences that involve practice and perception, such as: learning, listening to and singing a song, playing hand games or circle games. Thus, through the development and understanding of these activities, children reach increasingly sophisticated levels, as they begin to master these contents, allowing them to transform and recreate them. The RCNEI highlights music as an important part of the child's development and learning process, which is allied to body movement:

Gesture and body movement are linked and connected to musical work. It involves both gesture and movement, because sound is also gesture and vibratory movement, and the body translates the different sounds it perceives into movement. The movements of bending, balancing, twisting, stretching etc., and those of locomotion such as walking, jumping, running, hopping, galloping etc., establish direct relationships with the different sound gestures (BRASIL, 1998, p. 61).

As such, movement becomes a strong ally in the teaching and learning of music and, as we shall see later, dance also plays a role in learning and culturally identifying certain styles of music.

In addition to what we have already shown, music teaching can contribute not only to the students' musical education,

[...] but mainly as an efficient tool for social transformation, where the teaching and learning environment can provide the respect, friendship, cooperation and reflection that are so important and necessary for human formation. [...] (SOUZA E JOLLY, 2010, p. 100).

For this to happen, we can see that musical content must be developed in music classes for children, but other skills such as socialization, affectivity, creativity, imagination, communication, among others, will also be worked on simultaneously. According to the RCNEI:

The integration of sensitive, affective, aesthetic and cognitive aspects, as well as the promotion of social integration and communication, give musical language its significance. It is one of the most important forms of human expression, which in itself justifies its presence in the context of education in general, and in early

24

childhood education in particular (BRASIL, 1998, p. 45).

2.3.3 Dance as an expressive and corporal language in Early Childhood Education

One fact that cannot be denied is that children are in constant movement, which contributes to their learning and development, as we have already shown. Another type of movement that adds to a child's learning and development is dance.

Dance is a strong ally for learning about new cultures and recognizing our own. It is one of the four artistic languages that should be covered in the school curriculum, and the fourth to be recognized as an area of knowledge. We know that the teaching of art was made compulsory in basic education by Law no.

9694/96 states: "Art teaching will be a compulsory curricular component at the various levels of basic education, in order to promote the cultural development of students" (art. 26). However, its introduction in schools is still recent, thus generating the understanding that dance has its own signs, where these own signs can be observed in the contextualization of dance as well as in its history and in the experience of dance itself, that is, the elements that make it up, such as repertoires, improvisation and choreographic composition.

The language of dance at school can provide close contact with local culture, in the sense of broadening the observation of ways of dancing and perceiving the body in **movement**, drawing up new aesthetic possibilities, rescuing body histories and building many others. In addition to local culture, dance can provide children with contact with new cultures.

Dance allows children to build different ways of relating to themselves, to others and to the socio-cultural environment. In other words, dancing is not just about rehearsed movements, but about building self-knowledge, affection, interaction with others and respect for oneself and others.

The National Curriculum Framework for Early Childhood Education (BRASIL, 1998) includes dance as part of the movement axis, and through this we can develop a new concept, which goes hand in hand with what has already been said, that dance is bodily expression and social reading, which motivates and creates sustainable awareness. In the RCNEI:

Human movement, therefore, is more than just moving the body in space: it is a language that allows children to act on the physical environment and act on the human environment, mobilizing people through its expressive content (BRASIL, 1998).

Expression through movement accompanies human development and life. These movements can express feelings, emotions and intimate states, which vary according to the culture and its way of expressing itself.

25

In order for dance teaching to provide new learning opportunities for children, Verderi (2009) states that:

Dance at school should provide opportunities for students to develop all their human behavioral domains and, through diversification and complexity, the teacher should contribute to the formation of more complex body structures.

Therefore, it is up to the teacher to stimulate the contents of this body culture, promoting the formation of cognitive, motor and socio-affective processes, which can arouse students' interest in the educational process.

Dance provides a moment in which we can touch our inner selves, through the senses, reading the world with a new language, so that education fulfills its full function. It is in Early Childhood Education that we can provide better dance learning and enable children to develop fully, because everything is penetrated through contact with the world through their bodies. However, the teaching of dance should not just be restricted to nursery school, but to the whole of primary education.

In addition to movement, music and dance as multiple languages presented by children, we have one that is inevitable when we talk about childhood/children: *play*. Play is the language we use to identify childhood and through it it is possible to understand the cultural context in which the child is inserted. It is also through play that we can observe the different languages they use, as if they were in tune with each other. In play, we can bring together music, movement, dance and speech.

2.3.4 Play: expression of multiple languages - pleasure and learning

Another source of learning for children is play. We can say that play opens up multiple windows of interpretation, understanding and action on reality for the child. Through play, children can reproduce real situations, modify things and objects, invent and carry out actions and interactions with the help of gestures, expressions and words, they can go back in time and become a gentleman, a princess and even a dragon. And this is possible thanks to the child's inexhaustible source of imagination, where most of the time children act guided by it and by the meanings created and shared with their peers.

When children play, they are not only expressing and communicating their experiences, but they are also reworking themselves, recognizing themselves as subjects belonging to a social group and a cultural context, where they represent the social relationships and cultural meanings present there. As Borba (2006, p.47) states "[...] play is therefore an experience of culture, through which values, skills, knowledge and forms of social participation are constituted and reinvented by the collective action of children".

In this way, play is a cultural phenomenon, as it is configured together with a set of practices and

26

knowledge produced, constructed and accumulated over time, an example of which is that we can still see children playing hopscotch, ring toss, ciranda, marbles and other games that their grandparents played when they were children. Borba (2006, p.47) points out that:

By playing with others and taking part in playful activities, children build up a repertoire of games and cultural references that make up children's play culture, i.e. the set of experiences that allow children to play together (BROUGÈRE, 2002). In other words, play culture makes play possible, but it is in the social space of play itself that it also emerges and is enriched.

As a result, we can say that children learn by playing alone, with each other and with adults, and this play is born, reborn and enriched. Adults and children pass on the prevailing cultures based on the cultural references they have built up, and Borba (2006) adds that as children develop, they appropriate this form of social action and the cultural collection of games historically built up in their social context. The author states:

From an early age, children develop situations of interaction with their elders, which are essential ways of learning to play. Adults' games of hiding under pieces of cloth or other screens, and then surprising babies by finding them, are examples of this type of playful interaction. The baby's expressions of contentment encourage the play to continue and, gradually, the baby takes on a more active role, also taking on the role of the adult. The child learns to recognize certain defining characteristics of play: the fictional aspect, because the person doesn't really disappear, it's make-believe, on a different plane from immediate reality; repetition, which shows that you can always go back to the beginning, without reality changing; the need for the partners to agree to play together and an absence of consequences and commitment to results, because it's more important how you play than what you're looking for (BORBA, 2006, p.48).

It is therefore possible to state that play is a source of rich knowledge that can be passed on to the child, without the need to tell the child what they are learning or developing. So we ask ourselves: why is play often excluded from the classroom, given that it can only add to the child's learning? We believe that the reason for this "exclusion" is due to the fact that teachers and educators find it difficult to link play, learning and the subject curriculum, so that one doesn't interfere with the other. But according to Moyles (2006, p.15), "a simple model of the curriculum for nursery and primary education indicates that there need not actually be any conflict of interest, as each element is readily interwoven with the others. [...]".

In addition to a simple but structured curriculum, ensuring that each aspect is intertwined, it is necessary to stress that when play is introduced into the classroom, educators need to structure the field of play in children's lives, making objects, fantasies, toys or games available and providing space and time to play, as stated by the National Curriculum Reference for Early Childhood Education - RCNEI (BRASIL, 1988).

According to Piaget (1951), play is extremely characteristic in the age group of 2 to 6 years. For the author, play is divided into: **practical play**, **symbolic play** and **games with rules**. Practical play takes place between the ages of 6 months and 2 years and basically includes the baby's sensory-motor and exploratory play. Symbolic play takes place between the ages of 2 or 3 and 6 and includes make-believe, fantasy and dramatic play. Finally, there are games with rules, which are characteristic of the play/activities of children aged 6 to 7. It's important to note that a large part of a child's play will be symbolic, since children reinvent an action or object by distorting the meanings they would have in "real life".

But how can we understand children's play behavior? According to Moyles (2006, p.16), many educators use the model of play created by Corinne Hult (1979). The model developed by Hult consists of a division of play into three categories: *epistemic behavior*, playful *behavior* and *play with rules*. According to Moyles (2006), to explain epistemic play, Hult relies on the fact that children explore various materials and gain knowledge and manipulative skills, which is a prerequisite for the development of other knowledge and skills. The playful elements of play, which include the way in which children engage in make-believe, allow for more opportunities and creativity in linguistic play and are opportunities for rehearsal and practice. Play through games, on the other hand, takes place at increasing levels of difficulty and limitation determined by rules and incorporated into simple social games, for example, number games and riddles.

However, there are not only these types of play, but also free play. In free play, the teacher lets the children choose how and with what they want to play, thus bringing not only fun but also learning through the child's free choice. However, it is worth pointing out that some free play can become repetitive, so it is recommended that educators try to help children develop their play. Adults can stimulate, encourage or challenge children to play in a more developed way, but the tasks they are asked to perform must be within their competence and age range.

When playing, children acquire social and physical skills. As *already mentioned, a* large part of play is social, because when children are playing with each other they are socializing and interacting. In addition, many theorists claim that play brings various intellectual benefits, because through play children are not just learning to learn, they are learning about themselves.

Playing prepares children for the future, allowing them to experience the world around them. It is through play that situations perceived or experienced by the child take on new meaning. The school environment must be conducive to these interactions between the child and the object they have chosen. It is this exchange and interaction between them that will allow them to construct and deconstruct concepts permeated by a mixture of reality and fantasy.

Play is a benchmark and an objective that must be followed and implemented in school planning, as it is recognized by the National Framework for Early Childhood Education, as well as the other topics presented here. Play unleashes a whole process of magic, colors and movements that help to develop the whole individual. Children need the opportunity to explore the world, to investigate, to understand when to play, developing their motor, emotional and cognitive capacities, and in short, to develop fully. Playing is an essential part of pedagogical action, generating the pleasure of learning pointed out in the National Framework for Early Childhood Education:

In early childhood education institutions, children can be offered conditions for learning that takes place through play and learning that comes from intentional pedagogical situations or learning guided by adults. [...]. Educating therefore means providing situations of care, play and learning that are guided in an integrated way and that can contribute to the development of children's capacities for interpersonal relationships, for being and being with others in a basic attitude of acceptance, respect and trust, and children's access to broader knowledge of social and cultural reality. [...] (BRASIL, 1998, p.23).

Thus, because of the need for play and its action in everyday school life, children not only form their knowledge naturally, but also have the opportunity to experience playful and pleasurable situations. In this way, play enables the child, during their development, to be able to relate adequately to the world around them, first in an imitative way and then in an increasingly personal and creative way, allowing them to achieve autonomy.

Recognizing play and its role in children's learning is not necessarily a problem. Several educators and researchers have given countless examples and varied evidence that play is the child's way of learning and that to neglect or ignore the role of play as an educational medium is to deny the child's natural response to the environment. Therefore, play is, and should be, the right of all children, because as we have seen, through play children are also learning many skills and concepts, and this is a way for educators and teachers to transmit new ways of learning to children.

2.3.5 The language of drawing: visual art used by children

If we analyze the origins of drawing, we'll see that it was already present in ancient history through cave paintings. We can therefore say that drawing is a language that has been built up over the years. As Derdyk (1990, p. 10) states:

Man has always drawn. He has always left graphic records, indices of his existence, intimate communications destined for posterity. Drawing, such an ancient and permanent language, has always been present, ever since man invented man. It has crossed spatial and temporal boundaries and, because it is so simple, it stubbornly accompanies our adventure on Earth.

In this way, we can describe drawing as a universal language, which is linked to society and culture and spreads over several generations. It is a language that has its own peculiarities and history.

According to Junqueira Filho (2005), drawing is a language with its own structures and rules in which it transmits any and all human achievements, fitting into a system of representation as a production of meaning. By drawing, children imprint records and therefore express and communicate.

Children also learn about their own humanity, insofar as when they draw, they are realizing - reaffirming and updating - something ancestral to their humanity: the ability and need of human beings to leave themselves in marks. It was human beings who invented drawing and, in doing so, they were able to say something about themselves through images, they were able to see themselves graphically represented in aspects of their humanity; they left themselves in marks that contributed to the production of their humanity, of their history; that contributed to the demarcation, communication and significance of their passage through life, through planet Earth, through the world (JUNQUEIRA FILHO, 2005, p. 54).

Thus, we can say that drawing is also a graphic sign, as Derdyk (1990, p. 101) points out: "The graphic sign is the result of an action charged with intentionality, not yet fully expressed. The eye, spectator of this conversation between hand, gesture and instrument, perceives forms".

With regard to drawing being a sign, the National Curriculum Framework for Early Childhood Education (BRASIL, 1998) points out that drawing as a language indicates historical and social signs that enable man to signify his world.

By drawing, children convey their wishes, desires and unleash their imagination, representing life as they see it. As a result, it's impossible not to see a child with a pencil in their hand drawing, whether at school or not, so it's almost impossible not to find houses and schools with drawn walls, floors and even the children themselves. According to Derdyk (2004) drawing expresses experience and becomes a form of play that generates pleasure.

The first drawings are made for the pleasure of scratching something, whatever the surface. To justify this statement, we rely on the following excerpt:

Children scribble for the pleasure of scribbling, of gesturing, of improving themselves. The graphism that emerges from this is essentially motor, organic, biological and rhythmic. When the pencil slides across the paper, the lines appear. When the hand stops, the lines don't happen. They appear, they disappear. The permanence of the line on the paper is invested with magic and sensorially stimulates the desire to prolong this pleasure (DERDYK, 2004, p.56).

Drawing is not only pleasurable, it's also a game, because when drawing, in addition to the sensation of pleasure, the child plays with the drawing and with their classmates, they unleash their imagination when drawing and create stories with their drawing. Therefore, the act of drawing is also social, as the child interacts with other people to show and tell what they have drawn.

For Hanauer (2010), drawing as a language can be considered an instrument of knowledge that allows children to travel new paths and take ownership of the world around them.

30

The child who draws establishes relationships between their inner and outer worlds, acquiring and reformulating concepts and improving their abilities, involving themselves affectively and operating mentally. They externalize (*sic*) feelings and express thoughts (HANAUER, 2010, p.5).

With all that said, we can't talk about drawing without describing the stages it goes through, so we sought support from Vygotsky's ideas on drawing. According to Vygotsky (1991), the development of drawing requires two conditions: motor mastery and the relationship developed with existing speech when drawing. Vygotsky (1991, p.141) states that verbal language is the basis of graphic language and classifies the development of expression, which he calls graphic-plastic, into the following stages:

I) **Symbolic stage** - This is the stage of the well-known puppets that represent, in a way

in short, the human figure. This stage is described by Vygotsky as the moment when children draw objects "from memory" with no apparent concern for fidelity to the thing represented.

II) **Symbolic-formalist stage** - This is the stage in which we can already see a greater elaboration of the lines and shapes of children's graphs. This is the period in which the child begins to feel the need to go beyond merely listing the concrete aspects of the object they are representing, seeking to establish a greater relationship between the whole represented and its parts, and we can already see the beginnings of a representation that is closer to reality.

III) **True formalist stage** - In this stage, the graphic representations are faithful to the observable aspect of the objects represented, with the more symbolic aspects present in the previous stages coming to an end.

IV) **Plastic formalist stage** - A new form is identified, a new way of drawing, because as a development of motor skills, drawing ceases to be an activity with an end in itself and becomes creative work. However, there is a slowing down of the pace of drawing, which remains more among those who really draw because they enjoy this creative act.

When describing the developmental stages of children's graphism, the author doesn't bother to detail the period of acquisition of the drawing representation system. We can therefore say that drawing is one of the most important bases for analyzing the child's progress. Its development contributes to symbolic representation, motor and emotional development and consequently to learning as a whole.

31

3. METHODOLOGICAL ASPECTS OF THE RESEARCH

We began our work by talking about the history of childhood and the invisibility it has suffered over the years, presenting the acquisition of language as perceived by Vygotsky

(1993) and Tomasello (2003) and, finally, we report on the multiple languages presented by the children. We have done all this because we believe that our object of study includes the discussions raised so far.

Our research, a subproject of a larger PIBIC/UEPB (Scientific Initiation Program) project - 2016/2017 - on Children's Languages in the Pedagogical Practice of Early Childhood Education Institutions, had as its basic purpose the analysis of conceptions and uses of languages in pedagogical practices by teachers who work in some institutions that offer this basic stage of education.

Our quantitative and qualitative research took place in two public nursery schools in different municipalities. One of them, located in the municipality of Alagoa Nova (Creche Professor Clodomiro Leal, located in Rua Severino de Assis Mathias, Alagoa Nova - PB, 58125-000) and the other in the municipality of Campina Grande (Creche Alcides Cartaxo Loureiro, located in Rua R. Geralda de Fàtima Paiva Maia, 399-525 - Très Irmas, Campina Grande), both in the state of Paraiba. The subjects involved were teachers who work with children aged 0 to 3 in these institutions. Our project was submitted to the Ethics Committee of the State University of Paraiba (located at Rua Baraùnas, 351 Universitàrio, 2° andar, sala 214) and all the subjects involved signed a consent form for the data to be published and disseminated. Both institutions that participated in our project were authorized by their representative bodies, the municipal education departments (attached is the consent form sent by the Campina Grande municipal education department).

As a data collection tool, we used questionnaires with six open questions. We sought to analyze the data provided through the studies of Bardin (1979) on content analysis.

With regard to the discussion and analysis of the data, we drew inspiration from Bardin's (1979) Method of Content Analysis, although we did not define the categories of analysis based on the answers to the questionnaire applied to the teachers involved. For Bardin (1979, p.31), this method is defined as "[...] a set of techniques for analyzing communications. "In other words, content analysis seeks to ascertain what a given text is trying to convey by studying everything from the way it is written to the intention behind the text. Because the intention behind content analysis "[...] is to infer knowledge about the conditions of production (or possibly reception), an inference that uses indicators (qualitative or not) (BARDIN, 1979, p.38).

In addition to the intention behind the question, it is necessary to understand that in content analysis there are two types of problems: What led to a particular statement? According to Bardin (1979, p.39) "[...] this aspect concerns the causes or antecedents of the message". In our case, what led us to carry out the research, through the statements in the questionnaire, was the fact that we wanted to understand and explore the conceptions of the teachers who work in Early Childhood Education, with children aged 0 to 3, about the multiple languages that are presented by the children.

The second problem: what consequences is a given statement likely to have? Here Bardim (1979) considers the possible effects that will be caused by the message. In addition to investigating multiple languages, our intention was to encourage teachers to discuss the subject and to show the academic community the importance of multiple languages for children's development.

However, when using content analysis as an analytical tool, it is important to consider the links between "the surface of the texts, described and analyzed (at least some characteristic elements) and the factors (sic) that determined these characteristics, deduced logically" (BARDIN, 1979, p.40). For [...] what is sought to be established when an analysis is carried out, consciously or not, is a correspondence between the semantic or linguistic structures and the psychological or sociological structures of the statements. [...]".

In other words, content analysis goes beyond just analyzing the written text, it seeks to investigate the link between the semantic or linguistic structures and the psychological or sociological structures present in the statements/answers, since the psychological and the social interfere in the way we view the world.

Finally, Bardin (1979, p.42) designates the term content analysis as:

A set of communication techniques aimed at obtaining, through systematic and objective (sic) procedures for describing the content of messages, indicators (qualitative or not) that allow the inference of knowledge regarding the conditions of production/reception (inferred variables) of these messages.

Content analysis has various analysis procedures, so we opted for the analysis of answers to open questions. According to Bardin (1979, p.60), when analyzing a questionnaire with open questions, one can opt for two distribution procedures. The first starts from the *general* to the *particular,* "[...] the classification headings are determined first and then an attempt is made to organize the whole. " (Idem), in other words, you start with small parts and then begin to organize the answers to arrive at the final result.

The second is precisely the opposite "[...] we start from the particular elements and progressively regroup them by approximating contiguous elements, so that at the end of this procedure we assign a title to the category" (BARDIN, 1979, p.61). The first procedure was used to analyze our research.

We also used categorization, which for Bardin (1979, p.117) is an action of classifying characteristic elements of a set. By differentiation and then by regrouping according to genre (analogy), with previously defined criteria. Furthermore, categorization is a structuralist process and involves two stages: "*inventory*: isolating the elements; *classification*: dividing up the elements, and thus seeking to impose a certain organization on the messages" (BARDIN, 1979, p.117, emphasis added).

Thus, using Bardin's (1979) categorization, we divided our results into two categories: in the first category we sought to analyze the profile of the teachers involved in our research; and in the second we sought to explore the teachers' conceptions and practices in relation to multiple languages.

As already mentioned, the collection instrument used was a questionnaire with open questions, which we designed and which was sent to and approved by the UEPB Research Ethics Committee. It was a questionnaire containing the identification data of those being investigated, with six open questions. A total of thirteen questionnaires were answered and handed in, which served as the basis for this work.

The data that was collected is laid out in informative surface graphs in the Microsoft Office Excel 2016 program. Therefore, the main objective was to collect real data on the understanding of the teachers involved about language and the multiple languages used by children.

4. Analysis and discussion of results

The field research involved questionnaires answered by teachers who work in Early Childhood Education with children aged 0 to 3. Following the methods presented by Bardin (1979), we used classification to better discuss the results. The teachers' profiles and six categories were catalogued, in which we sought to address children's language and multiple languages.

4.1   Profile of the teachers

To construct this category, we used the following data: training and length of time working in Early Childhood Education. We will not use gender as a categorical data since all the questionnaires were answered by female teachers.

4.1.1 Training

It can be seen in this category that most of the teachers who agreed to answer our questionnaire only have a degree in Pedagogy, around 44%. The other 14% were teachers with a normal school education (magisterium) and a post-graduate degree in Early Childhood Education. There was an equal result of 7% between those with a degree in normal school/graduate degree in Pedagogy, graduate degree in Pedagogy, graduate degree in another area and those who did not wish to state their degree.

Graph 1: Teachers' level of education

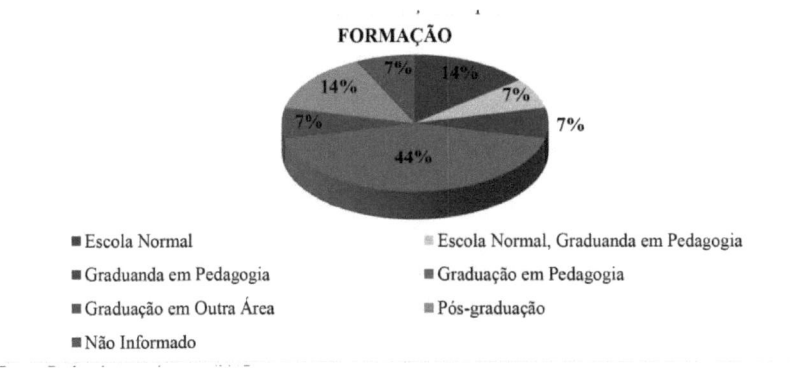

Source: Survey data, Mar/2017.

4.1.2 Length of time working in Early Childhood Education

In this dimension, we tried to analyze the length of time teachers have been working in the Early Childhood Education classroom. By analyzing the graph, it was possible to see that 46% of the teachers have been working in the classroom for between 7 and 10 years. Another percentage that caught our attention was that of those working between 15 and 25 years, which was 38%. Again, there was an equal percentage, 8% for those who had been working for between 1 and 6 years and 8% who did not tell us.

Graph 2: Length of time working in the Early Childhood Education classroom

ATUAÇÃO NA EDUCAÇÃO INFANTIL

8%   8%

38%   46%

■ 1 a 6 anos   ■ 7 a 10 anos   ■ 15 a 25 anos   ▪ Não informado

Source: Survey data, Mar/2017.

4.2 Language and multiple languages

We divided our results into six categories where we focused on the language and multiple languages presented by the children. These six categories are: What is language; Multiple languages that are observed in children; Languages used by children in teacher-child interaction; Languages used by children in child-child interaction; Exploration of languages in teachers' planning; and finally the teachers' view of monitoring the development of some languages.

4.2.1. What is language?

This item was formed from the first question on the questionnaire, which was: "How do you define language?" Despite being a simple question, we could observe a certain difficulty on the part of the teachers in answering, since their answers were short and some lacked meaning, with a view to a better understanding. We obtained the following data: 50% of the teachers said that language was a means used to communicate and interact with each other, 25% said it was a way of expressing oneself, 17% described it as verbal and non-verbal language, and 8% described language as the representation of sound through speech.

By constructing the graph, it was possible to see that the majority of teachers define language as a means we use to communicate and express ourselves, which can be verbal (through speech) or non-verbal (through gestures, music, etc.). This understanding, although limited, is supported by the perspective of language presented by Vygotsky (1993) and Tomasello (2003). However, it is also

36

possible to observe that many teachers still define language only as a system of symbols or the representation of speech sounds.

Graph 3: What is language?

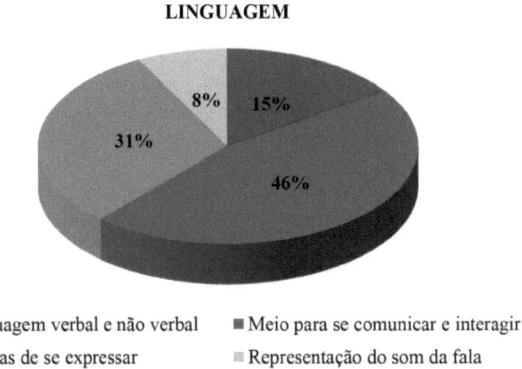

Source: Survey data, Mar/2017.

4.2.2. The multiple languages that are observed in children

The purpose of this item was to understand the teachers' ideas about multiple languages and how they observe them in children. As the questions are linked to each other, but with different objectives, it was possible to analyze that the teachers had a certain difficulty, because despite the question being simple, 15% limited themselves to answering only yes, which led us to wonder if the teacher really understands what multiple languages are presented by children and their importance, or due to the short time they only answered yes.

However, 46% of the teachers said that children do have multiple languages and that they are used through verbal language, drawing, music and movement. And 31%, in addition to what had already been mentioned, also cited children's crying and babbling as multiple languages. Finally, 8% said that the existence of multiple languages is limited to verbal and non-verbal forms.

Graph 4: The multiple languages presented by the children

AS MÚLTIPLAS LINGUAGENS

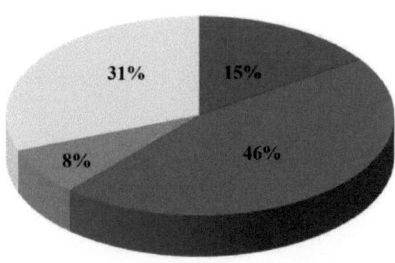

■ Sim
■ Sim, através da linguagem verbal, do desenho, da musica e do movimento
■ Sim, linguagem verbal e não verbal
■ Sim, utilizam os gestos, balbucios, imagens e o choro

Source: Survey data, Mar/2017.

4.2.3. Languages used by children in teacher-child interaction

In this section, we tried to explore the interaction between the teachers and their children and which languages were used by the children during this interaction. 31% of the teachers said that the children use verbal and non-verbal language and specified some of the times when they are used, such as in games and proposed activities. Around 23% said that children use speech, facial expressions and body language. A further 23% specified socializing and playing.

However, 15% of the teachers said that children use gestures, looking and crying. For these teachers, we hypothesize that they work in the nursery with children under 1 year old, because as we have seen, before children acquire speech, they use gestures, looking and crying to communicate. And 8% specified oral language as the only means of language.

Graph 5: Languages used by children in teacher-child interaction

38

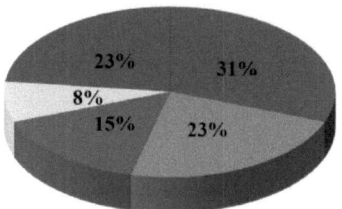

INTERAÇÃO PROFESSORA-CRIANÇA

23%   31%
8%
15%   23%

■ Linguagens verbais e não verbais, por meio de brincadeiras e atividades propostas
■ A partir da socialização e do brincar
■ Com o gesto, com o olhar e o choro
 Apenas a linguagem oral
■ Através da fala, das expressões faciais e corporais

Source: Survey data, Mar/2017.

4.2.4. Languages used in child-child interactions

Unlike the other item, in this one we tried to explore which languages were used by the children in child-child interactions and in which situations the teachers observed these interactions. We found that around 39% of the teachers noticed this interaction in the games played by the children, and this only affirms what has already been said, since when children play they are learning about themselves, others and their own culture.

We noticed that 23% of the teachers observed this interaction through oral and body language. As we discussed earlier, when quoting the RCENEI, children use various forms of communication, thus the multiple languages they use or present, body language can be considered one of these languages, as the aforementioned Referencial Curricular para Educaçao Infantil (BRASIL, 1998, vol. 3, p.47) points out,

The ways of walking, running, throwing and jumping are the result of social interactions and human relationships with the environment; they are movements whose meanings have been constructed according to the different needs, interests and human bodily possibilities present in different cultures at different times in history.

And a further 23% said that this relationship occurred through touch, looking and babbling between the children. Again, we believe that these teachers work in nursery classes and that they try to include multiple languages in their planning.

Finally, 15% observed that the languages used by the children in their interactions with each other were verbal language, movement and representation.

In this section we have tried to show that children learn from each other and through various languages, and that they do not depend solely on the teacher or any other adult for learning to take place. As stated in the National Curriculum Framework for Early Childhood Education (RCNEI), emphasized here again, it is necessary for Early Childhood Education to promote integration between the physical, emotional, affective, cognitive and social aspects of children aged 0 to 5, considering them as complete and indivisible beings, as well as giving them access to socio-cultural goods, essential care for the development of their identity and the right to play as a particular form of expression, thought, interaction and communication.

Graph 6: Languages used in child-child interactions.

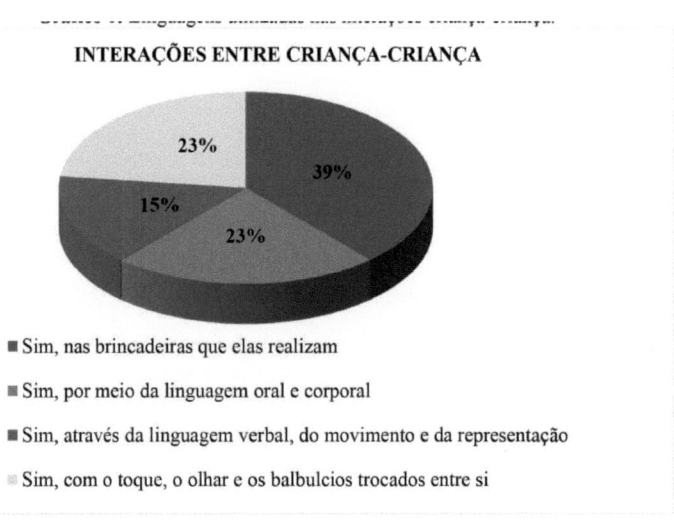

INTERAÇÕES ENTRE CRIANÇA-CRIANÇA

- Sim, nas brincadeiras que elas realizam
- Sim, por meio da linguagem oral e corporal
- Sim, através da linguagem verbal, do movimento e da representação
- Sim, com o toque, o olhar e os balbucios trocados entre si

Source: Survey data, Mar/2017.

4.2.5. Language exploration in teachers' planning

The aim of this item was to find out whether the teachers used multiple languages in their planning and which ones they used most. According to Graph 7, around 54% of the teachers said that they use multiple languages in their planning and always include oral and body language, drawing, play and dance. In contrast, 38% reported that they included oral, musical and visual language in their planning. Finally, 8% said that they use oral language through reading and storytelling, and music that uses gestures during its melody.

We know how important it is to plan lessons. In Education

When planning the activities that will be developed, the teacher needs to take into account multiple languages, since we have already made their importance for the development of the child as a whole very clear. It is necessary to remember that the nursery teacher is a mediator of knowledge, as the RCNEI states:

The intervention of the teacher is necessary so that, in the early childhood education institution, children can, in situations of social interaction or on their own, expand their capacity to appropriate concepts, social codes and different languages, through the expression and communication of feelings and ideas, experimentation, reflection, the elaboration of questions and answers, the construction of objects and toys etc. [...] In the early childhood education institution, the teacher is therefore the most experienced partner par excellence, whose role is to provide and guarantee a rich, pleasurable, healthy and non-discriminatory environment for varied educational and social experiences (BRASIL, 1998, Vol. 1, p.30).

It is therefore the role of the nursery school teacher to provide activities that encourage and develop children's multiple languages. Respecting their limitations, their culture and the pace of their development. We were pleased to see that the teachers who agreed to answer our questionnaire consider the multiple languages presented by the children in their planning.

Graph 7: Multiple languages in teachers' planning

AS LINGUAGENS NO PLANEJAMENTO

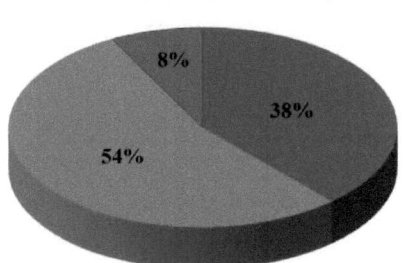

■ Sim, contemplamos a linguagem oral, a musical e a visual

■ Sim, contemplamos a linguagem oral e corporal, o desenho, o brincar e a dança

■ Sim, contemplamos a linguagem oral (por meio da contação de história) e das musicas que utilizam gestos

Source: Survey data, Mar/2017.

4.2.6. Accompanying teachers in the development of certain languages

The main objective of this item was to find out whether the teachers considered it important to monitor the development of certain languages and what these languages were. We obtained a percentage of 41% of the teachers saying that they monitor the development of languages in their children, which are: oral language, gesture, movement and drawing. 33% said they monitor the development of oral, body and musical languages. 16% said they only monitored oral language. And finally, 10% reported that they monitor the development of multiple languages, but did not specify which languages these were.

Teacher supervision is of fundamental importance at any level of education. However, in Early Childhood Education this work needs to be carried out with extra attention, since we are dealing with children who are in a constant process of learning and development. Since

The teacher **mediates between the children and the objects of knowledge**, organizing and providing learning spaces and situations that articulate the affective, emotional, social and cognitive resources and capacities of each child with their previous knowledge and with the contents of the different fields of human knowledge (BRASIL, 1998, Vol.1, p.30 - emphasis added).

Graph 8: Teachers' support for the development of certain languages

Source: Survey data, Mar/2017.

In the course of our work, we present the emergence of the feeling of childhood and the (in)visibility it has suffered over the years. We made this journey because in order to understand childhood it is necessary to know its history, it is of the utmost importance to know our past so that mistakes are not repeated, We did this so that the concepts of language developed by Vygotsky (1993) and Tomasello (2003) could be presented, as both discuss language and its acquisition and development from a socio-cultural perspective, where it is stated that the acquisition and development of language occurs from the social to the individual.

Finally, we discussed the multiple languages that children display, whether they are in the process of acquiring them or developing them. All of this was of fundamental importance for the data presented in the research to be presented, because through our research it was possible to observe that although teachers observe multiple languages in their children and are aware of their importance for children's development, it was noticed that many teachers still focus on the development of verbal language, although they consider movement, drawing and so on to be languages that are rarely contemplated in their planning, in the activities developed and in the monitoring that must be carried out.

5. FINAL CONSIDERATIONS

We have tried to establish a link between the History of Childhood, starting with the highlighting of the feeling of childhood exposed by Philippe Ariès (2011), and its sociological contexts, addressing the (in)visibility suffered by childhood over the years, presented through the ideas of Sarmento (2007). We made this connection because we believe that it is of fundamental importance to know the history of childhood in order to understand the childhood that is present today. There is no point in focusing only on the present without understanding what happened before, since the whole concept of childhood was historically constructed. If we recall what was initially presented by Ariès (2011), we will see that the childhood we know today was constructed to serve the society of a certain time and that it developed so that we would have the idea of the child that is presented in our society today: the child who plays, studies and is supported by the family and by various laws and entities.

This historical bridge was necessary for us to understand the idea of language developed by Vygotsky (1993) and Tomasello (2003), since both elaborate their theories of language acquisition and development from the concept that not only the biological factor is responsible for language acquisition and development, for them the historical, social and cultural factors are, together with the biological, responsible for its development.

It's important to point out that despite having the same idea of how the process of acquisition and development takes place, the authors have their own distinctions in their theories. As presented when discussing Tomasello's theories (2003), in addition to the factors mentioned above, there is also joint attention, a key concept for understanding the process of language acquisition and development from Tomasello's point of view.

Finally, we went through all this to introduce the multiple languages. Throughout the work, we made it clear that the concept of language adopted here was that any form of communication that conveys intention and meaning is considered to be language. Since our study was carried out with kindergarten teachers who work with children aged 0 to 3, where verbal language is almost absent, we need to know that children use other languages.

Although verbal language is one of the languages most used by children, it is not the only one. In order to communicate, convey what they are feeling, interact with society and on other occasions, children use multiple languages. It is necessary for teachers to understand this so that multiple languages are included in planning and that the teacher is able to develop in the child not only verbal language, but all the languages necessary for children to develop as a whole.

The survey showed that the conceptions of language adopted by the teachers are the same as those that appear in their planning and teaching practices. For example, when teachers say that language is a form of verbal and non-verbal communication, they restrict their planning/practice to the use of oral language and drawing, forgetting that other languages need to be developed in order for the child to develop fully.

It is worth noting that movement, dance, music, drawing and play are languages that appear in the National Curriculum Framework for Early Childhood Education, so they need to be worked on in early childhood education institutions. They deserve to be worked on with the child not just as a pretext to complement the activity carried out in the morning, in other words, there needs to be a sense, a plan, so that they are worked on in a way that is meaningful for the child's development and learning.

Finally, we would like to emphasize that multiple languages need better attention from teachers, because it is up to them to develop a rich linguistic vocabulary in their children, not just orally, but in the broad sense of multiple languages.

REFERENCES

AFONSO, Maria Aparecida Valentim. **Children's musicality:** discovering the sounds of the body, objects and the world. In:_ BARBOSA, Rita Cristina; AFONSO, Maria Aparecida Valentin (org.). Educaçao Infantil: das prâticas pedagógicas às politicas pùblicas. Joao Pessoa: Editora Universitària da UFPB, 2011. p.109-128.

ÀLLAN, Sylvio. SOUZA, Carlos Barbosa Alves. **Tomasello's model of human cognitive-linguistic evolution.** Psicologia: Teoria e Pesquisa, Brasilia, Apr-Jun 2009, Vol. 25 n.2 pp.161-168.

ARIÈS, Philippe. **História social da criança e da familia.** 2.ed -Rio de Janeiro: LTC, 2011.

BAKHTIN, M. (V. N. Voloshinov) **Marxism and philosophy of language.** Trad. M. Lahud and Y.F. Vieira. Sao Paulo: Hucitec, 1988.

BRAZIL. Ministry of Education. Department of Basic Education. National Policies for Early Childhood Education. Brasilia, 2006.

BRAZIL, Ministry of Education and Sports. Department of Basic Education. **Referencial Curricular Nacional para Educaçao Infantil.** Brasilia: MEC/SEF, v. 3. 1998

BORBA, Ângela Meyer. **Play as an experience of culture.** In:_ O cotidiano na Educaçao Infantil. Bulletin 23, November 2006. P. 46-55

DERDYK, Edith. **Drawing the human figure.** Sao Paulo: Scipione, 1990.

. **Formas de pensar o desenho:** desenvolvimento do grafismo infantil. 3. ed. Sao Paulo: Scipione, 2004.

GARANHANI, Marynelma Camargo. **The body in movement in Early Childhood Education: a child's language** In. V EDUCERE - III CONGRESSO NACIONAL DA ÁREA DE EDUCAÇÃO, 5. 2005. Curitiba. *Proceedings...* Curitiba, 2005. p. 2017-2025

GALVÂO, Izabel. **Henri Wallon:** a dialectical conception of child development - Rio de Janeiro: Vozes, 2008.

GIL, Antônio Carlos. **How to design research projects.** 5.ed. Sao Paulo: Atlas, 2010.

HANAUER, Fernanda. **Scratches and doodles:** drawing in early childhood education. Ideau education magazine. Vol. 6 - N° 13 - January - July 2011.

JOBIM E SOUZA, Solange. L.S. **Vygotsky: language and the social construction of consciousness.** In: ___ Childhood and language: Bakhtin, Vygotsky and Benjamin. Campinas, Sao Paulo : Papirus, 1994 (p.123 - 136)

JOLY, Ilza, Zenker, Leme, (2003). **Education and music education:** knowledge for understanding children and their relationship with music. In:. HENTSCHKE, L; DEL BEN, L. (Orgs.). Teaching music: proposals for thinking and acting in the classroom. Sao Paulo: Ed. Moderna. Chap. 7.

JUNQUEIRA FILHO, Gabriel de Andrade. **Generative languages:** selection and articulation of content in early childhood education. Porto Alegre: Mediaçao, 2005.

KUHLMANN JR., M., FERNANDES, R. **On the history of childhood.** In: FARIA FILHO, L. M.(Org.). A infância e sua educaçao: materiais, pràticas e representaçoes (Portugal e Brasil). Belo Horizonte: Autêntica, 2004, p.15-33.

MELO, Glória Maria Leitao de Souza. **Language and its acquisition:** interactionist approaches. In: __ Scenes of joint attention between teachers and children in the process of language acquisition. 2015, 276 p. Thesis (Doctorate)

MOYLES, Janet R. **The excellence of play:** the importance of play in the transition between early childhood education and the early years. Porto Alegre: Artmed, 2006.

OLIVEIRA, Marta Kohl. **Vygotsky:** learning and development, a socio-historical process - 4. ed. Sao Paulo: Scipione, 2002.

PALOMO, Sandra Maria Silva. **Language and languages**. Eccos Scientific Journal. Sao Paulo: Centro Universitàrio Nove de Julho, v.3, n.2, p.9-15, dec.,2001.

SARMENTO, Manuel Jacinto. **Social visibility and the study of childhood**. In.

_ VASCONCELLOS, Vera Mª Ramos de. SARMENTO, Manuel Jacinto (org.). Infância (in)visivel. - Araraquara, SP: Junqueira&Marin, 2007.

SOUZA, Carlos Eduardo de. JOLLY, Maria Carolina Lima. **The importance of music teaching in Early Childhood Education**. Cadernos da Pedagogia. Sao Carlos, Ano 4 v. 4 n. 7, p. 96 - 110 , jan -jun. 2010

VYGOTSKY, Lev. Thought and language. 5ª reprint. Sao Paulo: Martins Fontes, 1987.

VYGOTSKY, Lev. The social formation of the mind. 4th edition. Sao Paulo: Martins Fontes, 1991.

VERDERI, E. **Dança na escola:** uma abordagem pedagógica. Sao Paulo: Phorte, 2009.

WALLON, Henri. **Psychology and Childhood Education**. Translated by Rabaça, Ana. Lisbon: Estampa, 1975.

. **Psychology and education of the child**. Lisbon: Veiga, 1979.

APPENDIX A - CONSENT FORM

INFORMED CONSENT FORM

Dear Teacher

The research entitled: CHILDREN'S LANGUAGES IN SOCIAL INTERACTIONS OF JOINT CARE IN THE CHILDHOOD AND THE FAMILY, approved by the Scientific Initiation Program (PIBC) of UEPB/CNPq, is being developed by Sayonara Ramos Marcelino Ferreira Quirino (matric: 111215170), Giszélia Oliveira dos Santos (matricula: 131218735) and Simone Fernandes de Melo (matricula:131211510), under the coordination and guidance of Prof. Dr. Glòria Maria Leitner. Dr. Glòria Maria Leitâo de Souza Melo, professor at the Education Department of the State University of Paraiba. The aims of the study are To investigate the multiple languages used by children in contexts of social interactions of joint attention with the adult, in the nursery and in the family, in order to better understand the communication established by them and the construction of these languages, from an early age; To identify in the process of acquisition of the child's oral language, other languages apprehended/constructed and expressed by them; To analyze the spaces offered in the nursery and in the family, for the exploration of multiple languages by the children; To discuss teachers' conceptions of language, of children's languages, and of their pedagogical practices in exploring these languages; To identify the use of languages by children in social interactions of joint attention, as well as the understandings and meanings they attribute through their languages; To observe whether the acquisition/construction of orality is driven by social interactions of joint attention and by the use of other forms of language; To analyze the role of the other (adult or child) in the process of acquisition/construction of languages by the child.

The research is longitudinal in nature, and the data will be collected in two public nursery schools located in the urban area of Campina Grande - PB, involving children aged between 0 and 03 years, and the teachers who work in these institutions. The data will be collected over a period of 4 (six) months, every 15 days, through video recordings and interviews, according to the daycare center's shifts.

This is a study that will bring benefits to pedagogical and curricular practices in early childhood education, with a view not only to the process of children's acquisition of spoken language, but also to the various possibilities they have for using and expressing multiple languages in contexts of social interaction and joint attention. To this end, we would like to ask for your cooperation in: authorizing filming in your class; granting a pre-prepared interview; and authorizing the presentation and publication of the results of this research at scientific events, in books, magazines or annals related to the humanities and social sciences, either in printed or digital form.

As for the risks of this research, they are summarized in the possibility of exposing the oral manifestations of children and teachers, which occur through interactions in the school environment, if we consider them as discourses of subjects.

Finally, the researcher/coordinator can be contacted for any clarifications by calling (83) 3331-5799/988585051; and by e-mail: profgmls@hotmail.com.

In view of the above, I declare that I have been duly informed and give my consent to participate in the research and to publish the results. I am aware that I will receive a copy of this document.

Campina Grande, _____ de _____ de _____

Teacher   Researcher

Witness

Researcher's address: R. Tabeliao Severino de Lacerda, 40 Catolé - Campina Grande - PB

Address of the UEPB Ethics Committee: R. Baraûnas, 351 Universitario, 2° andar, sala 214, fone:33153373

E-mail: cep@uepb.edu.br

APPENDIX B - QUESTIONNAIRES USED

QUESTIONNAIRE WITH OPEN QUESTIONS

target audience: nursery and pre-school teachers

FIELD OF RESEARCH: public institutions in Alagoa Nova - PB and Campina Grande - PB.

Identification data:

- Full Name: _____

- Training: _____

- Institution you work for: _____

- Time working in Early Childhood Education: _____

Questions:

1. How do you define language?

2. Do you think children have multiple languages? Why?

3. According to your teaching experience, what languages are used by

children during your interactions with them?

4. What about the interactions between the children themselves? What languages are most

observed by you?

5. Do you include language exploration in your planning?

children? Are there any more contemplated? Which ones?

6. Do you consider it important to monitor the development of some

languages? Why? What are these languages?

ANNEX A - OPINION OF THE ETHICS COMMITTEE

STATE UNIVERSITY OF
PARAíBA

PRO-RECTORY OF POSTGRADUATE STUDIES AND RESEARCHER
ETHICS COMMITTEE FOR RESEARCH INVOLVING
HUMAN BEINGS
NATIONAL ETHICS COMMITTEE FOR RESEARCH INVOLVING
HUMAN
BEINGS
BRAZIL PLATFORM

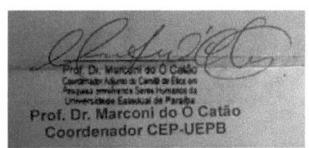

Prof. Dr. Marconi do Ó Catão
Coordenador CEP-UEPB

Research Title: CHILDREN'S LANGUAGES IN SOCIAL INTERACTIONS OF JOINT CARE IN THE CHILDHOUSE AND THE FAMILY. **Principal Investigator**: Prof. Dr. GLÒRIA MARIA LEITÀO DE SOUZA MELO **CAAE**: 6499516.0.0000.5187

PROJECT STATUS:

APPROVED. Rapporteur's date:

22/02/2017

Presentation of the Project: Project sent to the Research Ethics Committee of the State University of Paraiba, for analysis and opinion for the purpose of elaboration and development of research, in compliance with the PIBIC/UEPB/CNPq Notice, Quota 2016/2017, of the State University of Paraiba.

General Research Objective: To investigate the multiple languages used by children in contexts of social interactions of joint attention with adults, in the nursery and in the family,

51

in order to better understand the communication they establish and the construction of these languages, from an early age.

Assessment of Risks and Benefits: According to CNS/MS RESOLUTION 466/12, all research with human beings involves risks of varying degrees. This project has minimal risks, characterized as "embarrassment to participants or interruption of their time". However, these risks will be minimized by the ethical commitment of the researchers, and by the benefits of the research, which could have an impact on the curricular and pedagogical practices of institutions that care for children aged 0 to 5, in the sense of looking at how to reshape some of these practices, making them more effective in the exploration and development of children's oral language and other languages that these children learn, construct and express in the social interactions of joint attention that they participate in, whether at school or at home.

Comments and Considerations on the Research: As the research protocol is a set of documents describing the research in its fundamental aspects, the current project complies with the criteria and guidelines of CNS/MS Resolution 466/12.

Consideration of mandatory terms: The necessary and mandatory terms are present.

Recommendations: No recommendations.

Conclusions or Outstanding Issues and List of Inadequacies: The project is complete, with no outstanding issues. In view of the above, we are in favor of approval.

Campina Grande, February 22, 2017.

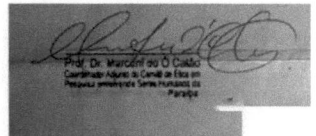

ANNEX B - LETTER OF CONSENT

Ilma. Sra. Iolanda Barbosa Silva

Com o objetivo de realizarmos o projeto de pesquisa, intitulado: **LINGUAGENS DAS CRIANÇAS EM INTERAÇÕES SOCIAIS DE ATENÇÃO CONJUNTA NA CRECHE E NA FAMÍLIA,** solicitamos vossa autorização para coletarmos dados, junto a crianças e professoras das seguintes instituições de Educação Infantil: CAIC José Joffily, localizada no bairro das Malvinas e a Creche e Pré-Escola Alcides Cartaxo Loureiro, localizada no bairro do Cinza. A coleta de dados será feita através de filmagens e de entrevistas. Esclarecemos que a investigação não trará custos para as referidas instituições, nem provocará alterações em suas rotinas pedagógicas.

Campina Grande, 08 de setembro de 2016.

Atenciosamente,

Glória Maria Leitão de Souza Melo – Mat. 1234013
Profa. Responsável/Orientadora do PIBIC

Giszélia Oliveira dos Santos
Aluna/orientanda – Mat. 131218735

Simone Fernandes de Melo
Aluna/orientanda – Mat.131211510

AUTORIZAÇÃO:

Iolanda Barbosa da Silva
Seccretária de Educação do Município de Campina Grande – PB.

Printed by Books on Demand GmbH, Norderstedt / Germany